WORKBOOK
FOR

ATOMIC

HABITS

AN EASY & PROVEN WAY TO BUILD GOOD HABITS & BREAK BAD ONES

By

JAMES CLEAR

PockeTBooks

Table of Contents

HOW TO USE THIS WORKBOOK

This workbook is designed to guide readers into breaking bad attitudes and embracing good behaviours. Readers will have an understanding of how they can make a positive change in their lives by putting in little and consistent daily routines. Readers can make a positive change in their lives if they read this workbook carefully and follow the guides and instructions of the workbook.

In the book **"Atomic Habits" by James Clear,** James guides us through a simplified and well explained steps/pattern through which readers, learn how they can become a better version of them self. This workbook, helps you put those steps into motion by pushing you to not just read, but take action. To get the best out of the book, and life itself, answer the questions, apply the lessons and follow the action steps provided in this workbook.

The lessons contained herein are easy to understand and the **action steps guide the reader** aright as he employs the lessons learnt. With **the checklist**, the reader is set on the perfect path, being prevented from digressing but simply adhering to all that this workbook has to offer.

A diligent, true, committed answering of the questions would open the reader up to a world of bliss, and expose him to areas hitherto untouched. The reader can be sure that their expectation for picking up the workbook is met.

Have fun, be patient with yourself, and enjoy using this workbook.

INTRODUCTION

The book, Atomic Habits by James Clear is loaded with tips on how readers can change their habits for good. It opens their eyes to the power of little changes and how these changes can mold readers into a better version.

This workbook is what you need for your daily guide. It will help you to improve yourself and personality. It's more than just a workbook; it shows the correlation between your attitudes and your identity. This workbook will show the readers the importance of steadiness and consistency in building habits that projects their identity positively. Atomic Habits workbook is all you need to work on your habit and reshape your identity.

Why Tiny Changes Make a Big Difference

Chapter 1: The Surprising Power of Atomic Habits

We tend to appreciate the defining moments of life than the little improvements we make on a daily basis. Many times we believe that great achievements require significant actions. This belief and idea are what make us mount unnecessary pressure on ourselves. We always think of making that ground-breaking improvement before we can be convinced that we are improving. Meanwhile, we neglect our little daily improvements. James Clear, in his book 'Atomic Habits' describes the little daily improvements as 1 percent improvement.

The truth is, 1 percent improvement goes a long way and can lead to more significant achievements in life. James Clear said, "If you can get 1 percent better each day for one year, you'll end up thirty-seven times better by the time you're done. Conversely, if you get 1 percent worse each day for one year, you'll decline nearly down to zero."

Habits are known to be the accumulation of our self-improvement. We seem not to count on the little changes we make daily, forgetting the fact that its consistency and duplication daily is what brings the result. For instance, if you visit the gym for three straight days, you won't see any result yet. You don't have to give up because you didn't see the result within three days, you have to keep working out to get in shape. The daily input you are making until you achieve your desired body is the 1 percent improvement you are making.

A little shift in your daily habits can lead you to a different destination in life. If the regular shifts are positive shifts, then you are on the way of becoming successful. But if it's a negative shift, then you are on the path of destruction. Your current situation doesn't matter, the point here is whether you are contributing something positive daily toward becoming your best and being successful in life.

James Clear said, "Your outcomes are a lagging measure of your habits. Your net worth is a lagging measure of your financial habits. Your weight is a lagging measure of your eating habits. Your knowledge is a lagging measure of your learning habits. Your clutter is a lagging measure of your cleaning habits. You get what you repeat." Everything has to do with your habits. Your habit is a major determinant of how you end up in life.

Habits can be likened to a two-edged sword. Bad habits can demote you while good habits can elevate you. It's essential for us to know the importance of habit and how to work on it to achieve success in life. As said earlier, habits are accumulated or compounded. There are two types of habit compounds. We have positive compounding, and we have negative compounding, and they both come with their impacts on our lives.

Positive compounding comes with knowledge compounds, productivity compounds, and relationships compound while negative compounding comes with negative thoughts compound, outrage compounds, and stress compounds. The big breaks we have in life are the results of the previous actions we've taken at one time or the other.

A lot of people focus on achieving a certain goal forgetting their attitudes determine if the goals will be achieved or not. It's better for us to work on our systems rather than setting goals. The system is the process through which a goal can be achieved. If the system is bad and not worked on, the goals will never be achieved.

Lessons & Takeaways
- We must understand that our habits play a significant role in our destination in life.
- Good habits project us on the path to success.
- There's power in the tiny changes we make daily.
- Not all goals will be achieved if the system is terrible.

Questions

- In your own understanding, what is Atomic Habit?

_____

_____

_____

_____

_____

_____

_____

_____

- What path is your habit leading you to?

_____

_____

_____

_____

_____

_____

_____

_____

_____

- Mention the two types of habit compounds.

_____

_____

_____

_____

_____

_____

_____

_____

- Why is it essential to focus on the system rather than goals?

_____

_____

_____

_____

_____

_____

_____

_____

_____

Action Steps

- Make a decision to give your 1 percent improvement daily.
- Focus on your systems and not goals.
- Focus on long-term about changing your habits.

Checklist

- Never give up on your tiny changes.
- Endeavor to monitor your progress.
- Be positive about the little you contribute you daily.

Chapter 2: How Your Habits Shape Your Identity (and Vice Versa)

It is challenging to change our habits. There are two reasons responsible for this; at times, we tend to leave the right thing to change by changing the wrong thing. The second reason is that we attempt to change our habits in a way that is wrong. Change can occur at three levels, known as outcomes, processes, and identity.

Changing your outcomes is the first level. This level has to do with changing your results. The goals you set to achieve fall in this category. Some of these goals can be reading a book, losing weight, winning a championship.

Changing your processes is the second level of change. This level has to do with changing your attitudes and systems. This is developing a new you by changing your habits. This level makes you take a deep thought about yourself, how and where you want to end up and start working on your ways.

The third and profound level of change is changing your identity. This level has to do with your personality. Your beliefs, judgments, self-image, and assumptions are all involved in this level. It's essential to know how and where to begin our habits changing process. Identity-based habits are highly important when considering changing our habits. This approach makes us focus on the personality we admire and wish to become.

A lot of people focus more on the outcome and process when considering changing their habits; they forget about identity change. They forget that their identity can be a threat to the new plans they have at hand. You may want a specific break, but your identity or personality may not give room for that particular break you desire. That's why it's essential to focus on changing our identity to accommodate future changes we want.

James Clear said, "The ultimate form of intrinsic motivation is when a habit becomes part of your identity. It's one thing to say I'm the type of person who wants this. It's something very different to say I'm the type of person who is this." When you start feeling proud of a specific area of your identity, you get the motivation needed to keep the habits active and sustained. The real change in behavior is identity change.

Identity change is focusing on the long-term result of our habits. You have to continually review yourself and your belief to become the best version of yourself. Your identity is the production of your daily habits.

Lessons & takeaways
- Identity change is essential.
- We have the power to believe whatever we choose to believe about ourselves.
- We must realize that no moment in life leaves us with no choice.

Questions

- What are the three levels of habit change?

_____

_____

_____

_____

_____

_____

_____

_____

_____

- How do you change your identity?

_____

_____

_____

_____

_____

_____

_____

_____

- What happens when you pride in a specific aspect of your identity?

_____

_____

_____

_____

_____

_____

_____

_____

_____

Action Steps

- Make a decision on the kind of person you desire.
- Focus more on the personality you desire.
- Create principles that will enable you to achieve your desired identity.

Checklist

- Be sure about the kind of change you crave and the one you are practicing.
- Focus more on the long-term in your habit change
- Don't be cynical about changing your habits.

Chapter 3: How to Build Better Habits in 4 Simple Steps

The process by which a habit is built can be categorized into four stages. The first stage is the cue, then we have the craving moment, the third is the response, and the last stage is the reward. These stages are the background of every habit, and it's in the same order that the brain operates per time.

The Cue: This is the first of the habit building process. There is a cue that puts your brain to work. It makes your brain to start processing the attitude to adopt, which in the long run will come with a reward. The reward in view is what determines the kind of habit your brain will initiate for that particular cue.

The craving: The craving stage is the second stage. It's the motivation that comes before every habit. The craving is what puts you to action. Your craving is not the habit but the sensation behind that particular habit. For instance; if you put on your television, what you crave is not putting on the TV; instead, you crave for entertainment from the TV. This is how your craving works.

The response: The response stage is the third stage of the habit building process. Your response is the exact habit you initiate. Your response can be in form of an action or thought. Your response is triggered by your motivation; how much you crave is what determines your response in a particular situation.

The reward: the last stage is the reward stage. This stage is what you get after your response. The reward is the product of every habit initiated. Rewards serve two goals for us; the first goal is the satisfaction we get after responding to a particular craving from a cue. The second goal is the teaching and experience we derive from the response.

The four stages of habits building can be divided into two phases. These phases are known as problem and solution phases. The cue and craving stages fall in the problem phase, while the craving and response stages fall in the solution phase. A willingness to solve a problem is what triggers every habit. That's where the cue and craving come into play. You put your brains to work here to find a way of solving the problem at hand. The response and reward represent the action taken to address the particular problem.

There are four laws of behavior change using the four stages mentioned above. The four laws of creating a good habit are as follows:

- Make your cue obvious.
- Make your craving attractive.
- Make your response easy.
- Make your reward satisfying.

You can also break bad habits using the same laws, but in a different way:

Make your cue invisible.

Make your craving unattractive.

Make your response difficult.

Make your reward unsatisfying.

Habits changing may be challenging at times; but if we apply these laws, in no time, we will see tangible results. These laws are applicable to almost all aspects of life.

Lessons & Takeaways
- Every habit has a price to be paid
- Our craving is what determines the response we initiate to every cue that comes to mind.
- The primary goal of habit is to proffer a solution to every problem at hand.

Questions

- Mention the four stages of habit changing process.

_____

_____

_____

_____

_____

_____

_____

_____

- List the four laws required to create good habits?

_____

_____

_____

_____

_____

_____

_____

_____

_____

- Mention the two stages of habit change associated with solution phase.

_____

_____

_____

_____

_____

_____

_____

Action Steps

- Endeavor to use your brain power to secure for yourself good habits.
- Always apply the four laws of habit change.
- At every point you need to make a decision, ensure you make the right decision with the right motive.

Checklist

- Be careful of the cues you entertain in your mind.
- Say no to bad habits.
- Never underestimate the laws of habit change.

Chapter 4: The Man Who Didn't Look Right

Our brains work like a machine that makes a prediction. It constantly absorbs and analyses the information and events it comes across. Whenever you have an everyday experience, your brain begins to focus on the crucial things from the experiences, sort them, and highlight them for future purpose. Your brain automatically encodes the lessons you derived from the experiences you have. Most times, it is difficult to state what we learn, but the truth is that we keep learning daily.

Our bodies and brains were created to do certain things for us on autopilot. For example, we don't tell our nails to grow, we don't say to our ears to hear, these things happen on their own, and we are not responsible for them. The surprising thing is that you don't necessarily have to be informed of a cue before a habit triggers. An opportunity can spring up, and you take action immediately without having to think about it. This is one of the usefulness of habits. Although there are two sides to it, it makes habits useful, and it makes habits dangerous, dangerous in the sense that if the habit is a bad habit.

As you form habits, some of your actions become automatic and comes from your non-conscious mind. With this, you tend to return to your old ways without knowing, unless your attention is called to it. We must be able to deal with our current habits before we can work on new ones. It can be challenging to handle, but once a habit is already a part of us, it triggers on autopilot. Carl Jung said, "Until you make the unconscious conscious, it will direct your life, and you will call it fate."

When we do a lot of things on autopilot, we forget to think about them. We overlook many things because we've done them frequently. We no longer question ourselves maybe those things we do on autopilot are actually right or wrong. Many of us fail in performance, and these failures are associated with our lack of self-evaluation and self-awareness.

Lessons & Takeaways
- The process of changing our habits begins with awareness.
- We must be aware of our habits before we can take steps to change them.
- Our brains a lot of actions automatically with repeated experience.

Questions

- What does your brain do when it encounters events repeatedly?

_____

_____

_____

_____

_____

_____

_____

_____

- What is the first thing to do if you want to build new habits?

_____

_____

_____

_____

_____

_____

_____

_____

- What did Carl Jung say about the unconscious?

_____

_____

_____

_____

_____

_____

_____

_____

Action Steps

- Devise means that you can use to help your self-awareness.
- Always take time out to evaluate yourself.

- Don't overlook the things you repeatedly do.

Checklist

- Don't underestimate your brain power.
- Never be too comfortable with a bad habit.
- Never stop paying attention to the things you do.

Chapter 5: The Best Way to Start a New Habit

The key here is 'implementation intention.' Implementation intentions are vital to being focused on our goals and achieving them. A typical example of implementation intention is "When this kind of situation arises, I'll give that kind of response to it." This is exactly how it works; it's a huge way to make us stick to our goals.

The truth is people who make plans ahead of a habit, and plan when, how, and where they will demonstrate it has better chances at succeeding with their plans. It's a deliberate and intentional act. A lot of people lack clarity, but they think what they lack is motivation. Lack of clarity doesn't make you know how, where, and when you should take action.

When your implementation intention is put in place, you don't need any motivation to get to work. The how, when, and where are already in place. All you have to do is stick to the plans already laid down plan. There are ways to apply the implementation intentions strategy. Below are two examples:

Exercise- I will work out for two hours at 4 p.m. in my local gym.

Meditation- I will be meditating for twenty minutes at 10 a.m. in my room.

The act, time, and location must be included in your plans. Another significant advantage of implementation intention is that it helps resist the things that derail your progress and the things that cause distraction. You need to create a time and also a space for your habits. Ensure you are specific enough with the location and time. Once it becomes a thing of repetition, you automatically start doing what is right at the right time. You won't be able to explain why and how you are doing it, but you naturally find yourself doing it. Jason Zweig said, "Obviously you're never going to just work out without conscious thought. But like a dog salivating at a bell, maybe you start to get antsy around the time of day you normally work out."

Lessons & Takeaways
- The best way to change our habits is through implementation intention.
- There's a need for us to be deliberate with our plans of changing our habits.
- Our habits could change if we give it time and space.

Questions

- What is implementation intention?

_____

_____

_____

_____

_____

_____

_____

_____

- State an example of implementation intentions strategy.

_____

_____

_____

_____

_____

_____

_____

_____

_____

- State one advantage of implementation intention.

_____

_____

_____

_____

_____

_____

_____

_____

_____

Action Steps

- Ensure you engage implementation intention to make changing your habits easier.
- Be deliberate about your plans.
- Resist whatever distracts your attention.

Checklist

- Watch out for the things that get you distracted.
- Say no to idleness.
- Never substitute your implementation intentions.

Chapter 6: Motivation is Overrated; Environment Often Matters More

Environment plays a significant role in changing our habits. Your habit responds to the cues before you and the environment you are. Specific environmental conditions mostly trigger some habits. For example, people tend to whisper in church, and we tend to behave protected in a dark place.

Vision remains the greatest of the sensory abilities in human. In the human body are up to eleven million sensory receptors, and up to ten million are devoted to vision. It is estimated by some experts that half of the resources in the brain are consumed on sight, it's proof that we as humans depend more on vision than other senses. With this understanding, our habits can be changed with a little change in the things we see. Imagine the essentiality of working and living in productive cues filled environment. The good news is, you don't have to remain your environment's victim, and you can create your environment to suit your progress.

You can recreate your environment and make obvious the signals that trigger the habits you desire. You can create a space in your environment for the cue needed to exhibit your preferred habits. For example, you can relocate your guitar stand to the center of your room if practicing guitar is what you desire. If you are interested in making a specific habit a huge part of your life, then you need to make the cue to the habit a huge part of your environment.

Lessons & Takeaways

- Our environment can play a significant role in our quest for new habits.

- Habits are triggered by cues, and we can make the signals obvious to encourage our preferred habits.

- The little changes we make in context can generate considerable changes in our habits with time.

Questions

- How can you recreate your environment?

_____

_____

_____

_____

_____

_____

_____

_____

- What is the connection between cues and habits?

_____

_____

_____

_____

_____

_____

_____

_____

_____

- Which of the sensory abilities is the greatest in a human body?

_____

_____

_____

_____

_____

_____

_____

_____

Action Steps

- Endeavour to create a good habit triggering cue in your environment.
- Give the cue time to win over your preferred habit for you.
- Recreate your environment to bring out the best in you.

Checklist

- Never remain a victim of your environment.
- Never underestimate the power of small changes.
- Be mindful of the environment you are.

Chapter 7: The Secret to Self-Control

The secret to self-control is not about being disciplined alone. There's more to it. The secret is to avoid tempting situations as much as we can. Self-control is not when you wish to be more disciplined. It's about creating for yourself a more disciplined environment. A habit that is already a part of you will always be on standby to trigger itself whenever the cue arises.

A long-abandoned bad habit, whenever an environment cue resurfaces, the habit tends to trigger upon sighting that specific cue. If cues are not well taken care of, we can unconsciously bring back the habits we have stopped or the ones we are trying to stop. Bad habits are self-triggering, and if the cues are not well controlled, we begin to crave for them.

It's easy to break a habit, but forgetting such a habit could be challenging. Once this behavior is already a part of us, it might be difficult for us to remove it entirely, regardless of when last we practiced such habit. Resisting temptations alone isn't the solution. We can overpower temptation, but it's aimed at the short-term. It's not sustainable for the long-term. The long-term goal to let go of bad habit is tackling bad habits to the source.

We can achieve this by controlling our access to the cues that cause such habits. The way we make the cues to good habits obvious, we can also make the cues to bad habits invisible. Once a wrong habit cue is removed, the habit would soon be gone and forgotten.

Lessons & Takeaways

- We can choose to avoid temptation rather than resist it.
- One of the most significant way to let go of bad habit is by reducing access to the cue.
- Self-control is only for short-term and not long-term.

Questions

- What happens when a habit is already a part of us?

_____

_____

_____

_____

_____

_____

_____

_____

_____

- From your understanding, what is the secret of self-control?

_____

_____

_____

_____

_____

_____

_____

_____

- What is the long-term strategy of changing bad habits?

_____

_____

_____

_____

_____

_____

_____

_____

Action Steps

- Make the cues to unwanted habits invisible.
- Deal with bad habits from the source.
- Aim a long-term elimination of bad habit and not the short-term.

Checklist

- Be mindful of the habit triggering cues in your environment.
- Be in control of your environment.
- Be careful of the things you crave for.

Make It Attractive

Chapter 8: How to Make a Habit Irresistible

The writer of the book, 'Atomic Habits,' James Clear said, "Make it attractive. The more attractive an opportunity is, the more likely it is to become habit-forming." Exaggeration is the order of the day in our society. The company advertising a product puts in all efforts, including Photoshopped edits, professional makeup, and lighting to make it attractive to you. Social media is continuously delivering exaggerated contents that are almost impossible in real life. This has become the norm in our society. Everything is presented to us with a high form of exaggeration, and we crave for them, thereby driven into extravagant shopping habits, social media habits, and lots more.

If you want to increase the chances of practicing a particular habit, there's a need for you to make that habit attractive. It's essential to learn how to make our habits more attractive to be irresistible. How can you make a habit irresistible? Temptation bundling is the key. It's by merely attaching a favorite craving to the behavior you intend to make a habit. This is what makes the habit irresistible to you.

For instance, if you want to get updated on celebrity gossips and also need to get in shape. You can adopt the temptation bundling strategy by reading the tabloids and watching TV shows at the gym. What you just did here is linking your wants with your needs. It works just like that, as you are having fun with what you want, you are also attending to what needs to be done. Even if you don't feel like doing what needs to be done, you'll be conditioned to doing it. Provided it's getting along with something you really want.

Lessons & Takeaways

- We can form new habits by making them irresistible.
- We can use what we want to get what we need.
- Temptation bundling goes a long way in making your habits irresistible.

Questions

- How can you make a habit irresistible?

_____

_____

_____

_____

_____

_____

_____

_____

- What is temptation bundling?

_____

_____

_____

_____

_____

_____

_____

_____

_____

- Mention two advantages of making a habit irresistible.

_____

_____

_____

_____

_____

_____

_____

_____

_____

Action Steps

- Key in to temptation bundling to maximize your preferred habit formation.
- Endeavor to align your wants with your needs to actualize your preferred habits.
- Be creative when implementing your temptation bundling.

Checklist

- Take note of the wants you engage when implementing your temptation bundling.
- Be careful of exaggeration.
- Never underestimate the possibilities of temptation bundling.

Chapter 9: The Role of Family and Friends in Shaping Your Habits

Charles Darwin said, "In the long history of humankind, those who learned to collaborate and improvise most effectively have prevailed." Human beings like to belong. We want to be like our family and friends. We want to do what they do and live the kind of life they live. Most times, we find it easy to move along with people. The urge to belong is ever increasing. If you grew with a set of people that compensate you for your football prowess, playing football will become very attractive to you.

Behaviors become attractive when it becomes a tool for us to fit in. The group of people whose habits we imitate are divided into three classes. We imitate the close, we imitate the many, and we imitate the powerful. The purpose of each class is to provide us with the opportunity to add attractiveness to our habit.

Imitating the Close

Closeness has a significant effect on us, and it influences our behavior a lot. We learn a lot from the people around us and emulate their habits as well. We copy a lot of things from our parents, our peers, and even our colleagues at work. We tend to imitate the habits of the people we are close to. One way to take advantage of this is to find a culture or group that exhibits the kind of culture we desire and join them. It will make it easier to blend in and make their habits a part of us.

Imitating the Many

Many times we are not sure what to do or how to act; we look at others to make our decision. We are always evaluating our environment and imagining what they could be thinking. At times we check the reviews on e-commerce sites to make our decisions. We do this because we aim to emulate the best buying habit. Although it could hurt an individual, the general opinion of the group might be lesser to the one the person has, the urge for acceptance will make us follow theirs.

Imitating the Powerful

Everyone pursues power. Everyone wants to be great and acknowledged. This is what draws us to people in power. We want to be the person giving the orders, and we want to be in charge wherever we find ourselves. This is why we crave the habits of the people in power.

Lessons & Takeaways
- Our culture tells on the habits that we find attractive.
- We can tap a lot from the people that are close to us.
- We find habits that grant us audience attractive.

Questions

- What are the three classes of habit we imitate?

_____

_____

_____

_____

_____

_____

_____

_____

_____

- What does it mean to imitate the close?

_____

_____

_____

_____

_____

_____

_____

- Differentiate between imitating the close and the many.

_____

_____

_____

_____

_____

_____

_____

Action Steps

- Find a culture whose habit attracts you and blend in.
- Follow up with the right team.
- Be open to learning new things.

Checklist

- Be careful about the kind of company you keep.
- Ensure you are imitating the right habit from the people in power.
- Don't always depend on people's approval.

Chapter 10: How to Find and Fix the Causes of Your Bad Habits

James Clear said," Every behavior has a surface level craving and a deeper, underlying motive." A craving represents the manifestation of our inner motive explicitly. Your brain was not created to crave Instagram or Facebook updates; that's you willing to belong for social acceptance. Some people see certain habits as a way of solving problems. For example, some smoke and drink alcohol to avoid thinking or reduce stress.

We associate certain habits to some things in life. Whatever we associate these habits with is what determine if there will be a repetition of the habits. Our habits are generated based on our reactions to happenings around us. Our interpretation of these events is what strikes our habits. These interpretations create different feelings, and these feelings create our cravings and desires.

The secret to fixing the cause of our bad habits is reframing our habits. A shift in our perspectives can transform our lives and how we live each day. James Clear shared an experience, "I once heard a story about a man who uses a wheelchair. When asked if it was difficult being confined, he responded, I'm not confined to my wheelchair—I am liberated by it. If it wasn't for my wheelchair, I would be bed-bound and never able to leave my house." These shifts in perspective go a long way in changing the feelings we relate with some of our habits. You can also design a motivation ritual around the habits you prefer and make it a cue to trigger such habits.

Lessons & Takeaways

- Every bad habit can be fixed; it all depends on our perspectives.
- We can stop a specific bad habit by making it unattractive.
- You can stop a bad habit by highlighting the advantages of avoiding it.

Questions

- What is a craving?

_____

_____

_____

_____

_____

_____

_____

_____

- How can you create a good habit?

_____

_____

_____

_____

_____

_____

_____

_____

_____

- How can you break a bad habit?

_____

_____

_____

_____

_____

_____

_____

_____

Action Steps

- Reframe your mind to accommodate your habits.
- Create motivation around your preferred habits.
- Create interest in the benefits attached to avoiding bad habits.

Checklist

- Continually check the prediction that precedes your habits.
- Take out time to evaluate your cravings.
- Check the things you associate your habits with.

Make It Easy

Chapter 11: Walk Slowly, but Never Backward

Many times we try to figure out a perfect plan for the change we desire. At times we get overwhelmed when we focus on the best strategy without taking actions. We often get in motion rather than taking actions. We get in motion by strategizing and mapping out plans which in the end without action is useless. Yes, being in motion is cool, but it needs an action to yield an outcome.

Most of us get in motion because we are scared of failure, we don't want to be criticized, and we want perfection in all things. Being in motion gives you a feeling that you are working things out and getting it done, but in fact, you are not doing anything. You are only making preparations.

If you want to form a preferred habit for yourself, you don't need to wait for perfection. All you have to do is begin with the repetition of the favorite habit. As the saying goes, "practice makes perfect." The key to habit formation is repetition. The more you engage an activity, the more your brain masters that activity puts it on autopilot.

It doesn't take long to form new habits. It only takes many to develop it. The 'many' in this context is the number of times you exhibit your habit. How many times you perform the habit is what determines its formation.

Lessons & Takeaways

- Practice is the best form of learning.
- It's better to take action than being in motion.
- Constant repetition helps habit formation.

Questions

- What is habit formation?

_____

_____

_____

_____

_____

_____

_____

_____

- Differentiate between being in motion and taking action.

_____

_____

_____

_____

_____

_____

_____

_____

- What is the key to habit formation?

_____

_____

_____

_____

_____

_____

_____

_____

Action Steps

- Be active with your plans.
- Take the bold step to begin the practice of your preferred habit.
- Have the courage to try something new.

Checklist

- Say no to procrastination.
- Don't be scared of failure.
- See criticism as an opportunity to improve yourself.

Chapter 12: The Law of Least Effort

It is generally accepted that the secret to habit change is motivation. Well, without motivation, we can change our habits if we really wanted it. The irony of it is that our real motivation lies in laziness and doing what is convenient. The human nature aligns with the Law of Least Effort. According to James Clear, the Law of Least Effort states that "when deciding between two similar options, people will naturally gravitate toward the option that requires the least amount of work."

The more energy required to perform a habit, the less likely it is for that habit to exist. But the less energy required, the more likely it is for that habit to materialize. If your ambition is to skip two thousand times a day, that requires a lot of energy, you might find it easy to do in the beginning because you are motivated to do it. But it feels exhausting after a few days, and just like that, that anticipated habit is gone. Meanwhile, if you stick to skipping five hundred times per day, you'd need little energy to get running. This is more likely to become a habit because it's not exhausting.

It's essential to simplify your habits so that it will be easy for you to do at any point in time. You don't have to motivate yourself to get used to a difficult habit. Instead, you can devise a strategy to reduce the friction attached to it. By practicing environment design, you can reduce the friction that is a potential threat to your preferred habits. As explained in chapter six, we can redesign our environment to align with our habits and make it easy to practice.

Lessons & Takeaways

- Habits become more practiced when we make it easier.
- Redesign your environment to help you practice the right habit.
- Reducing the friction associated with your preferred habits makes it easier to practice.

Questions

- Explain what you understand by the Law of Least Effort.

_____

_____

_____

_____

_____

_____

_____

_____

- How can you reduce friction when it comes to your preferred habits?

_____

_____

_____

_____

_____

_____

_____

_____

_____

- Mention one advantage of the Law of Least Effort.

_____

_____

_____

_____

_____

_____

_____

_____

Action Steps

- Redesign your environment to help you practice your habits more.
- Endeavor to simplify your habits.
- Ensure you reduce the friction that could sabotage your habits.

Checklist

- Don't become lazy while trying to simplify your habits.
- Be sure to get it right while redesigning your environment.
- Be careful with the strategy you adopt while practicing your habits.

Chapter 13: How to Stop Procrastinating by Using the Two-Minute Rule

Every habit needs one ritual or two to make it work. It is this ritual that makes it easy for us to practice such habits. For example, changing into your workout clothes when you come back from work. Instead of contemplating about working out, you have done the ritual by changing into your workout clothes. Once your cloth is on, there's the maximum assurance you'd be working out that day. This can be referred to as a decisive moment. The moment you make the decision to change into your workout clothes in anticipation of going to the gym.

According to James Clear, the Two-Minute Rule states that "When you start a new habit, it should take less than two minutes to do." Examples of a Two-Minute Rule are stated below;

"Do one hour of yoga" turns to "Bring out your yoga mat."

"Workout for two hours" becomes "Wear your workout clothes."

The essence of the rule is to soften your habits and make it a possibility to start. This is a strategy to get you started. Knowing that once you've begun performing the right habit, it won't be difficult to continue. With the Two-Minute Rule, it will no longer be challenging to form a new habit. The first two minutes of the journey will already be simplified. The Two-Minute Rule is the key to your gateway habits. The new habit you are about to start could be challenging, but your gateway habit will make it easier for the journey.

Every habit needs establishment before improvement comes in. The Two-Minute Rule is your aid in establishing your preferred habit, after which improvement follows through repetition.

Lessons & Takeaways
- A lot can be done in implementing our habits at decisive moments.
- The Two-Minute Rule is a huge boost to get us started with our preferred habit.
- Every habit can be improved once its practice has commenced.

Questions

- State the Two-Minute Rule.

_____

_____

_____

_____

_____

_____

_____

_____

- Mention one importance of the Two-Minute Rule.

_____

_____

_____

_____

_____

_____

_____

_____

_____

- Explain the meaning of a decisive moment.

_____

_____

_____

_____

_____

_____

_____

_____

_____

Action Steps

- Take advantage of the Two-Minute Rule to simplify your new challenge.
- Ensure you ritualize every process of your new challenge.
- Consider establishing your habits before improvement.

Checklist

- Never underestimate the possibilities of the Two-Minute Rule.

- Remember to take advantage of the ritual process for your next challenge.
- Keep your focus in the midst of starting your new habit.

Chapter 14: How to Make Good Habits Inevitable and Bad Habits Impossible

The best way to make our god habits inevitable and make the bad ones impossible is by adopting the strategy known by psychologists as commitment device. Commitment device leaves us with the choice we make now that controls our tomorrow. It's the best way to key in our future habit, makes us stick to good habits, and refrains us from bad habits. Commitment device makes you commit yourself ahead of time for a challenge you want to engage. It helps you to prepare yourself for what you intend to achieve, thereby leaving no room for falling into temptation. James Clear said, "Commitment devices increase the odds that you'll do the right thing in the future by making bad habits difficult in the present."

If you want to break a bad habit, the best way to go about it is to make that habit difficult to practice. You stretch and intensify the friction to the extent that you won't be able to practice such a habit. There are several ways you can use this device to key in with good habits. If you want to be more productive, you can cancel email subscriptions. You can delete some social media apps and games from your phone. If being happy is your goal, you can get yourself a dog. You can relocate to a social neighborhood. You can adopt the use of technology to ease a lot of difficult or stressful habits for you. The list is endless.

Lessons & Takeaways

- You can restrict yourself from bad habits by making it complicated.
- Good habits can be triggered by utilizing the commitment device.
- Habits automation goes a long way in aiding our new habits.

Questions

- Define the term commitment device.

_____

_____

_____

_____

_____

_____

_____

_____

- How can you make a good habit inevitable?

_____

_____

_____

_____

_____

_____

_____

_____

_____

- Mention two advantages of commitment devices.

_____

_____

_____

_____

_____

_____

_____

_____

Action Steps

- Make your bad habits so difficult for yourself.
- Endeavor to automate your habits to key in future activities.
- Employ the use of technology in actualizing your preferred habits.

Checklist

- Take advantage of the commitment device to secure the future.
- Watch how you use your commitment device.
- Ensure you commit your future to good habits.

Chapter 15: The Cardinal Rule of Behavior Change

It is easier to repeat an act when the encounter is satisfying. When you feel pleasured engaging a certain act, your brain gives you a signal of repetition. It gives you the cue to do more of the act. An unsatisfying encounter is less likely to be repeated. The Cardinal Rule of Behavior states, "What is rewarded is repeated. What is punished is avoided." Your experience in the past, be it reward or punishment determines what you'd do in the future. Positive feelings embrace habits, and negative sensations destroy them.

Every habit we practice generates several outcomes. Our bad habits make a good feeling immediately, but in the end, it's a bad feeling. The opposite is what goes for our good habits. Our good habits don't give a pleasurable outcome immediately, but at last, it gives a great feeling. When you overeat or have unprotected sex, they are acts you enjoy instantly, but the result is weight gain and a potential STD. It seems unenjoyable when you go to the gym to work on your body, but the result, in the long run, is pleasurable.

In other words, the penalty that comes with a good habit is in the present, and the punishment for a bad habit is waiting in the future. We tend to go with immediate pleasure when decision time pops up, and we tend to lose focus of our long-term ambitions. It's important to check ourselves if we are getting too much pleasure from our acts, and ask if we are doing the right thing. We should also note if those acts are following our future ambitions. We must always remember the Cardinal Rule of Behavior to guide our future.

Lessons and Takeaways
- Making a habit satisfying is a great way to practice it.
- A satisfying habit is more likely to be repeated.
- A good habit pays for long-term.

Questions

- State the Cardinal Rule of Behavior Change.

_____

_____

_____

_____

_____

_____

_____

_____

- What is the outcome of a habit that comes with immediate satisfaction?

_____

_____

_____

_____

_____

_____

_____

_____

_____

- What is the outcome of a habit that comes with a long-term satisfaction?

_____

_____

_____

_____

_____

_____

_____

_____

Action Steps

- Make use of the Cardinal Rule of Behavior Change as often as you can.
- Practice the habits that generate excellent outcomes.
- Focus on the long-term results of your habits.

Checklist

- Don't be too satisfied with habitual pleasures.
- Condition your brain to the kind of reward you want.
- Be careful about the kind of behaviors you put on repetition.

Chapter 16: How to Stick with Good Habits Every Day

When one is making progress with an act, it feels satisfying. When this progress is coupled with visual measures, the act triggers a habit with immediate satisfaction. The most effective way of measuring our progress is by tracking our habits. You can get a calendar to track your habit. If you read on certain days of the week, you can track your habit by marking each day you read. The phrase "Don't break a chain" is key to helping us in sticking to our preferred habits. When the phrase is always in your head, it makes you want to do more of the habit. Tracking your habit is essential; it helps you maximize the Laws of Behavior Change.

The benefits of habit tracking cannot be overstated. It is evident, satisfying, and attractive. Habit tracking is a massive way of motivating ourselves to do more. It breeds visual measures that serve as reminders for us to do more. It makes you satisfied after experiencing another day of productive habit. Not everyone can engage in habit tracking; some people see it as a habit on its own. They are struggling with the first habit, and adding habit tracking to it makes it overwhelming to them. The truth is, almost everyone can track their habit if they consider making it automated.

It's important to note that there will be times when you'll feel weary to continue with your habits. The whirlwind of life can strike at any time. The simple strategy to adopt here is a rule by James Clear, "Never miss twice." If you miss a day, do your best to get back to your habits as soon as possible. This rule another that works just like the "Don't break the chain" rule.

Lessons & Takeaways

- The sensation of making progress is highly satisfying.
- Habit tracker helps a lot in improving our habits.
- Nearly anyone can track their habits by embracing automation.

Questions

- What is habit tracking?

_____

_____

_____

_____

_____

_____

_____

_____

- Mention two benefits of habit tracking.

_____

_____

_____

_____

_____

_____

_____

_____

- What happens when you are making progress with an act?

_____

_____

_____

_____

_____

_____

_____

_____

Action Steps

- Endeavour to track your habits.
- Don't be overwhelmed trying to track your habits.
- Do well to maximize the Laws of Behavior Change

Checklist

- Don't break the chain.
- Never miss twice.
- Never give up.

Chapter 17: How an Accountability Partner Can Change Everything

We tend to repeat an act when the experience is satisfying, but when the experience is painful, we tend to avoid it. A painful failure gets fixed while a painless failure gets ignored. When a mistake is immediate and costly, we learn fast from it. The cost of a painful mistake makes a professional want to do his work as efficient as he can. So when the pain of an act is immediate and costly, we are less likely to repeat such a habit. The reason some bad habits are being repeated is because we derive pleasure from them, and that's why we find it difficult to stop them. The best way we can overcome them is by increasing the pace of the penalty attached to act.

We can hold ourselves accountable by embracing the use of habit contract. Habit contract, as stated by James Clear is, "A verbal written agreement in which you state your commitment to a particular habit and the punishment that will occur if you don't follow through." Once you've written this agreement, the next thing is to get the people that will serve as your accountability partners. It may be one person or two people. These people will officially sign the contract with you. The contract will contain your goals, how you plan to achieve it, and your daily activities toward achieving the goals. Included in the contract will be the punishment that follows if you refuse to keep up with the activities highlighted in the contract. You and your accountability partners will then sign the contract, and it will be strictly followed.

To overcome bad habits and make them unsatisfying, all you need to do is to associate those habits with immediate pain. A habit contract gives you the opportunity to discipline yourself to let go of bad habits.

Lessons & Takeaways

- We can let go of bad habits by making them unsatisfying.
- A habit contract can be used to stop bad habits.
- Accountability partners go a long way in quitting bad habits.

Questions

- What is a habit contract?

_____

_____

_____

_____

_____

_____

_____

_____

_____

- What is the role of an accountability partner in a habit contract?

_____

_____

_____

_____

_____

_____

_____

_____

_____

- Mention one advantage of a habit contract.

_____

_____

_____

_____

_____

_____

_____

_____

Action Steps

- Embrace a habit contract to help you quit bad habit.
- Ensure the punishments in your habit contract are strict enough to keep you off bad habits.
- State your goals clearly when writing your habit contract.

Checklist

- Be accountable for your habits.
- Evaluate and review your habit contract very well to ensure it's strict enough.
- Remember to make your bad habits unsatisfying.

How to Go from Being Merely Good to Being Truly Great

Chapter 18: The Truth About Talent (When Genes Matter and When They Don't)

If you want to be successful in life, you have to choose your field of competition wisely. This is precisely how it goes with habits. Habits become easily performed when they align with our innate abilities and natural inclination. The truth is, we are all created with different abilities. Our genes have their ways of naturally coming through for us in life. For example, if you want to excel in basketball, you need not be told that you have to be tall. You will have a lot of people and odds to contend with if you are short.

This is how our natural inclinations determine and influence our habits. Although your gene doesn't dictate your destiny, it influences areas where opportunities lie. The areas where you get a genetic boost for success are areas of habit satisfaction. The habits in these areas will be satisfying to you because you naturally fit into the areas. All you need to do is switch your focus to the areas you get excited and where you can exhibit your natural skills. The best way to identify the habits and opportunities that best fit you is by knowing yourself and understanding your personality.

Everyone has a unique image and personality. Your personality is broken down into five scopes of behavior. These series of behavior include; conscientiousness, openness to experience, neuroticism, extroversion, and agreeableness. These are the spectrums of behavior that describe our personality.

You can easily identify the habits that align with your gene when the habit seems easy to perform. If the habit sounds like fun to you while it looks like work to other people, you can tell your gene align with such a habit.

Lessons & Takeaways
- To be successful, you must choose your field of competition wisely.
- Choose the right habit to make the process easy.
- Our genes can also influence our habits.

Questions

- What is the key to success in life?

_____

_____

_____

_____

_____

_____

_____

- Mention three scopes of behaviour.

_____

_____

_____

_____

_____

_____

_____

_____

_____

- How can you identify the habits that align with your gene?

_____

_____

_____

_____

_____

_____

_____

_____

Action Steps

- Find a habit that aligns with your gene and maximize it.
- Choose a habit that you know suits you best.
- Create a game that excites you if you can't find one.

Checklist

- Observe your genes to know what best suits you.
- Identify yourself so as not to miss it in life.
- Embrace your gene and get the best of it.

Chapter 19: The Goldilocks Rule: How to Stay Motivated in Life and Work

Some of us, in one way or the other stick with our habits and keep practicing the habits while some of us find it difficult to stay motivated. James Clear said, "One of the most consistent findings is that the way to maintain motivation and achieve peak levels of desire is to work on tasks of just manageable difficulty." Our brains love challenges, but the kind of challenge the brain loves must be the one within its abilities. We tend to become tired of a challenge with too many odds against us but love the balanced one.

The Goldilocks Rule, by James Clear, states that "Humans experience peak motivation when working on tasks that are right on the edge of their current abilities." "Not too hard. Not too easy. Just right." When you are working on a new habit, you must simplify the behavior so that you will find it easier to stick with it even during difficulties. Once you have established the new habit, you'll keep on improving on it and keep yourself engaged till you strike the Goldilocks zone. A flow state is inevitable once you hit the Goldilocks zone the right way. A flow state is an act of being "in the zone" and completely engrossed with an action.

The Goldilocks Rule is all about engaging challenges with difficulties that are manageable. A challenge that is within your capabilities is essential to keeping you motivated. There will be times when you get bored getting things done. When you perform a particular habit every day, you get to a point where you get bored with the routine. This boredom makes us lose motivation and even gets some of us depressed. The solution to this is embracing variable rewards.

Variable rewards make the challenge or habits enjoyable, it won't come with an expected end, and the speed of rewards differs.

Lessons & Takeaways
- The brain tends to repeat habits with balanced challenges.
- Manageable challenges are more likely to occur.
- Failure is not the enemy of success, but boredom.

Questions

- State the Goldilocks Rule.

_____

_____

_____

_____

_____

_____

_____

_____

_____

- What is a state of flow?

_____

_____

_____

_____

_____

_____

_____

_____

- Mention one advantage of variable reward.

_____

_____

_____

_____

_____

_____

_____

_____

Action Steps

- Ensure your variable reward is in place for your next challenge.
- Continually push yourself to do more.
- Find motivation in your challenge.

Checklist

- Say no to depression.
- Prepare yourself ahead for the unexciting times of your challenge.
- Ensure your challenge is within your abilities.

Chapter 20: The Downside of Creating Good Habits

To pursue excellence in life, habit is the bedrock on which the possibility lies. However, there's a cost associated with the benefits of our habits. Once a habit is established, it becomes repetitive and goes automatic. This automation makes us careless of the feedbacks of our habits. We no longer become sensitive to the feedbacks of our habits. We become so lost in it that we don't think about how to correct the mistakes in our habits. The upside of our habits enables us to do things on autopilot. We can do it without having to think about what to do. As for the downside, we become so used to a specific way of doing things and stop focusing on the errors associated with it. Most times, we feel we are improving them, but we are actually not improving.

The way to salvage the situation here is to be deliberate with our automated habit. You can review your habits and make adjustments. You can look back after a period and review your habits over time. You can ask yourself what you did well, and reflect on the things that you didn't do well.

It's essential to keep our identity on a low profile, because of challenges that may arise in the future. It will be easy for us to remain ourselves and avoid depression or trauma. An identity that is highly placed and often become overwhelming makes it difficult for the personality involved to cope if any challenge rises in the future. For example, a footballer who is so successful and makes his identity so overwhelming won't be able to cope if he gets injured and unable to play football again. The idea is to be able to remain yourself when your identity or personality faces any challenge in form of the whirlwind of life.

Lessons & Takeaways

- The downside of our habits prevents us from improving our habit.
- The upside of our habits enables us to respond on autopilot.
- It's essential to reflect and review our habits over time.

Questions

- How can you review your habits and make adjustment?

_____

_____

_____

_____

_____

_____

_____

_____

- What is the effect of our habit upside?

_____

_____

_____

_____

_____

_____

_____

_____

_____

- Mention one importance of keeping your identity small.

_____

_____

_____

_____

_____

_____

_____

_____

Action Steps

- Continually review and reflect your habits over a certain period.
- Ensure to keep your identity low as much as you can.
- Take time out to correct the errors from your habits.

Checklist

- Be deliberate with your habit practice.
- Pay attention to the errors in your habits.
- Keep track of your identity.

CPSIA information can be obtained
at www.ICGtesting.com
Printed in the USA
LVHW100908220221
679617LV00008B/49